PASSOVER
&
PENTECOST

*Understanding the power
and purpose of passover and pentecost*

BISHOP DR. JOSEPH C. KANU

© 2022 Bishop (Dr.) Joseph C. Kanu

ISBN: 978-1-100-21782-6

Book cover design and Printing by
tmacre8tv@gmail.com
(+2348137371249)

Formatted by Framedwordsintl
(+2348139410461)

TABLE OF CONTENT

Acknowledgment

I wrote this book with the inspiration of the Holy Spirit and I want to give thanks to God for granting me the grace to write.

I also wish to use this opportunity to bless our Father in Heaven for His divine grace that eradicates shame and reproach and for how far He has brought me in a short while.

Dedication

I want to dedicate this book to The Holy Spirit because He is my source.

To my parents, siblings, family, children, mother in love, especially my wife who works behind the scenes for the success of our family and ministry.

To my Spiritual Father, church family, spiritual sons and daughters. I love you all.

Foreword

This book is in direct accordance
with the message given to me by
God. I personally wrote it down as a
sermon and a prayer book. The
purpose of this book is to shed more
light on the festival of Passover
which is the central Jewish
commemoration of the Israelite
exodus from Egyptian slavery. Its
spiritual significance is that it
signifies that we Christians are to be
servants of God who in return, will
bless us abundantly for our
obedience and faithfulness.

Furthermore, this book will also
show the connection between the
Pentecost and Passover and how that
connection can be a blessing to the

lives of we Christians. I pray that the good Lord bestows upon you blessings from above as you read through in the mighty name of Jesus, Amen.

The Power and Purpose of The Passover and
Pentecost

CHAPTER ONE

The Passover

Introduction

Well shall discuss in this chapter, the Judeo-Christian spiritual festival known as the Passover. We shall also shed light on its spiritual significance and importance.

What is Passover?

> *Exodus 12:14 (KJV) And this day shall be unto you for a memorial; and ye shall keep it a feast to the LORD throughout your generations; ye shall keep it a feast by an ordinance forever.*

The Passover, also known as the Hebrew *Pesaḥ* or *Pesach*, in Judaism, is a holiday commemorating the Hebrews' liberation from slavery in Egypt and the "passing over" of the forces of destruction, and the sparing of the firstborn of the Israelites, when the Lord *"smote the land of Egypt"* on the eve of the Exodus. Passover begins on the 15th and ends on the 21st (or, outside of Israel and among Reform Jews, the 22nd) day of the month of Nisan, which is either March or April on the Gregorian calendar. On these seven or eight days, all leaven, whether in bread or other mixture, is prohibited, and only unleavened bread, called *matzo*, may be eaten.

The *matzo* symbolizes both the Hebrews' suffering while in bondage and the haste with which they left Egypt in the course of the Exodus. Passover is also sometimes called the Festival of Unleavened Bread.

So put simply, the Passover (Hebrew: פסח, *Pesach*), is a religious holiday or festival noted by ceremonies each year, mostly by Jewish people.

They celebrate it to remember when God used Moses to free the Israelites from slavery in Egypt, as told in the book of Exodus in the Bible.

The Spiritual significance

Exodus 12:26-27 (KJV) And it shall come to pass, when your children shall say unto you, What mean ye by this service?

(27) That ye shall say, It is the sacrifice of the LORD'S passover, who passed over the houses of the children of Israel in Egypt, when he smote the Egyptians, and delivered our houses. And the people bowed their heads and worshipped.

1 Corinthians 5:7-8 (KJV) Purge out therefore the old leaven, that ye may be a new lump, as ye are unleavened. For even Christ our passover is sacrificed for us:
(8) Therefore let us keep the feast, not with old leaven, neither with the leaven of malice and wickedness; but with the unleavened bread of sincerity and truth.

The spiritual significance of Passover, based on the biblical interpretation, is one of salvation by the atoning blood of a perfect, spotless sacrificed lamb. For most Christians, this is the spiritual pattern seen in Passover which gives it its eternal meaning and significance. The theme is carried on and brought to its ultimate New Covenant fulfillment in the sacrificial death of Christ our Lord, as the promised sacrifice.

Why it's so important?

The Passover is important to we Christians because it is part of God's plan of salvation for us. With the exception of the Passover, the Jews would have perished as slaves in Egypt, Jesus might not have been born and, as a result, there would be no salvation for us.

Furthermore, the Passover is important because God ordained the Passover as a celebration of Jesus. 1 Cor. 5:7 says, *"Jesus is our Passover Lamb."* God could have had Jesus crucified at any time of the year, however, He chose to have Him die at Passover. God chose Passover because Passover was granted to teach us about Jesus. Through the Passover, we come to acknowledge what His death accomplished.

So in conclusion to this chapter, we have successfully shed light on what the Passover is, along with other relevant information on why we need to Observe this spiritual holiday.

I pray that the good Lord bless us abundantly as we proceed further in the mighty name of Jesus, Amen.

In the next Chapter, we shall shed light on the chosen man of God who greatly impacted the land of Egypt both naturally and spiritually.

> *The Passover is important to we Christians because it is part of God's plan of salvation for us.*

CHAPTER TWO

The story of Moses

Introduction

In this chapter, we shall discuss extensively the Prophet Moses and how he was called by God to deliver the people of Israel out of slavery. We shall also discuss the ten commandments and lessons we can learn from this influential man of God.

Who was Moses?

Moses, or as pronounced in Hebrew *Moshe*, was a Hebrew prophet, teacher, and leader who in the 13th century BCE (before the Common Era, or BC), delivered his people from Egyptian slavery.

Furthermore, in the Covenant ceremony at Mt. Sinai, where the Ten Commandments were promulgated, he founded the religious community known as Israel. As the interpreter of these Covenant stipulations, he was the organizer of the community's religious and civil traditions. In the Judaic tradition, he is revered as the greatest prophet and teacher, and Judaism has sometimes generically been called Mosaicism, or the Mosaic faith, in Western Christendom. His influence continues to be felt in the religious life, moral concerns, and social ethics of Western civilization, and therein lies his undying significance.

What he was known for

Moses is known as the most important and significant Jewish prophet. He's traditionally credited with writing the Torah and with leading the Israelites out of Egypt and across the Red Sea.

In the book of Exodus, he's born during a time when the Pharaoh of Egypt has ordered every male Hebrew to be drowned.

After Moses and the Jews leave Egypt, God gives him the Ten Commandments, which become the foundation of Jewish law and thought. For this reason, Moses is oftentimes referred to as the *law-giver*.

The Ten commandments

The Ten Commandments, also referred to as the *Decalogue* (Greek: *deka logoi* ["10 words"]), is a list of religious precepts that, according to various passages in Exodus and Deuteronomy, were divinely revealed to Moses on Mount Sinai and were engraved on two tablets of stone.

The Commandments are recorded virtually identically in Exodus 20:2–17 and Deuteronomy 5:6–21. The rendering in Exodus (King James Version) appears as follows:

Exodus 20:2-17 (KJV)
(2) I am the LORD thy God, which have brought thee out of the land of Egypt, out of the house of bondage.

(3) Thou shalt have no other gods before me.

(4) Thou shalt not make unto thee any graven image, or any likeness of any thing that is in heaven above, or that is in the earth beneath, or that is in the water under the earth:

(5) Thou shalt not bow down thyself to them, nor serve them: for I the LORD thy God am a jealous God, visiting the iniquity of the fathers upon the children unto the third and fourth generation of them that hate me;

(6) And shewing mercy unto thousands of them that love me, and keep my commandments.

(7) Thou shalt not take the name of the LORD thy God in vain; for the LORD will not hold him guiltless that taketh his name in vain.

(8) Remember the sabbath day, to keep it holy.

(9) Six days shalt thou labour, and do all thy work:

(10) But the seventh day is the sabbath of the LORD thy God: in it thou shalt not do any work, thou, nor thy son, nor thy daughter, thy manservant, nor thy maidservant, nor thy cattle, nor thy stranger that is within thy gates:

(11) For in six days the LORD made heaven and earth, the sea, and all that in them is, and rested the seventh day: wherefore the LORD blessed the sabbath day, and hallowed it.

(12) Honour thy father and thy mother: that thy days may be long upon the land which the LORD thy God giveth thee.

(13) Thou shalt not kill.

(14) Thou shalt not commit adultery.
(15) Thou shalt not steal.
(16) Thou shalt not bear false witness against thy neighbour.
(17) Thou shalt not covet thy neighbour's house, thou shalt not covet thy neighbour's wife, nor his manservant, nor his maidservant, nor his ox, nor his ass, nor any thing that is thy neighbour's.

What we can learn from him

The exodus story of Moses demonstrates justice through the Sinai covenant with God and Abram, which leads to the making of the ten commandments.

The story of Moses impacts today's society because through this, it shows us that even the most powerful of man has to have justice and to know when something is either right or wrong. Furthermore, below are other lessons we can learn from Moses:

- **Moses teaches us to see the possibility of miracles every day**

What would have happened if Moses hadn't noticed the miracle of that burning bush? He might have missed it along with his calling.

- **Moses teaches us about how to have a personal connection with God**

When God spoke to Moses out of that burning bush, he didn't question whether or not it was God speaking, he just entered into conversation with the voice that emanated from the bush. He accepted that the voice he heard was God's voice, and when God spoke, he answered.

- **From Moses, we learn that everyone has a destiny:** Moses had a destiny just like Joseph had a destiny. We are mostly in the right place at the right time even if it looks wrong.

- **Moses teaches us to be Assertive:** God keeps telling Moses repeatedly to go back to the Pharaoh and to say, "Let my people go." And he did, and eventually he got what he asked for. You have to ask for what you want.

- **Moses teaches us to have faith:** He must have had a lot of faith in God to go to the Pharaoh 10 times, and to lead the Israelites through the desert for 40 years, to simply do what God commanded. Moses' faith teaches us to act when God whispers in our ear or talks to us from a burning bush.

A man of redemption

Moses is also known as a man of redemption because that night God sent the angel of death to kill the firstborn sons of the Egyptians, God also told Moses to order the Israelite families to sacrifice a lamb and smear the blood on the door of their houses. In this way the angel would know to 'pass over' the houses of the Israelites. He is responsible for the salvation of every first born son of the Israelites that were in the land of Egypt

So in conclusion to this chapter, we can all acknowledge the works of this mighty man of God known as Moses and how we can learn significant lessons from his life.

CHAPTER THREE
The Ten plagues of Egypt

Introduction

We shall discuss in this chapter, the definition of plagues, what they are, their biblical references and their spiritual purposes. We shall also shed some light on how God used these plagues to free his people.

What are plagues?

Plagues can be defined as any contagious bacterial disease characterized by fever and delirium, typically with the formation of buboes (bubonic plague) and sometimes infection of the lungs

(pneumonic plague). Furthermore, a
Plague can also be an unusually large
number of insects or animals
infesting a place and causing
damage. Lastly, it can refer to a thing
or event that causes trouble or
irritation.

Biblical references

In certain places in the Bible, there is
mention of plagues, pestilence, or
pandemics killing people. For
example, in Lev. 26:25, when Israel
falls into covenant violations, God
says, *"I will send pestilence among you."*
In Second Chronicles 6:28, Solomon
says if there is pestilence, famine or
blight, may God hear from the
temple the prayers of the people. In
the next chapter, second Chronicles

7:13, God says that if he sends pestilence, the people can pray and humble themselves (verse 14)

Furthermore, the fourth Plague on the Egyptians is pestilence on their livestock, and as a result, they all die as mentioned in Exodus 9:3-6.

In second Samuel 24:15, God sends a pestilence that kills 70,000 Israelites because of David's ill-conceived census. Jesus says in Luke 21:11 that there will be plagues. Both Ezekiel and Jeremiah speak of God sending plagues, for example, in Ezek. 14:21 and 33:27, and Jer. 21:6-9. In Rev. 6:8, the "Pale Rider" kills a fourth of the earth with the sword, famine, and pestilence.

Leviticus 26:25 (KJV) And I will bring a sword upon you, that shall avenge the quarrel of my covenant: and when ye are gathered together within your cities, I will send the pestilence among you; and ye shall be delivered into the hand of the enemy.

2 Chronicles 6:28 (KJV) If there be dearth in the land, if there be pestilence, if there be blasting, or mildew, locusts, or caterpillars; if their enemies besiege them in the cities of their land; whatsoever sore or whatsoever sickness there be:

2 Chronicles 7:13-14 (KJV) If I shut up heaven that there be no rain, or if I command the locusts to devour the land, or if I send pestilence among my people; If my people, which are called by my name, shall humble themselves, and pray, and seek my face, and turn from their wicked ways; then will I hear from

*heaven, and will forgive their sin, and
will heal their land.*

*Exodus 9:3-6 (KJV) Behold, the hand
of the LORD is upon thy cattle which
is in the field, upon the horses, upon the
asses, upon the camels, upon the oxen,
and upon the sheep: there shall be a very
grievous murrain.*

*(4) And the LORD shall sever between
the cattle of Israel and the cattle of
Egypt: and there shall nothing die of all
that are the children of Israel.*

*(5) And the LORD appointed a set
time, saying, ``Tomorrow the LORD
shall do this thing in the land.*

*(6) And the LORD did that thing on
the morrow, and all the cattle of Egypt
died: but of the cattle of the children of
Israel died not one.*

*2 Samuel 24:15 (KJV) So the LORD
sent a pestilence upon Israel from the*

*morning even to the time appointed: and
there died of the people from Dan even
to Beersheba seventythousand men.*

*Luke 21:11 (KJV) And great
earthquakes shall be in divers places, and
famines, and pestilences; and fearful
sights and great signs shall there be from
heaven.*

*Ezekiel 14:21 (KJV) For thus saith the
Lord GOD; How much more when I
send my four sore judgments upon
Jerusalem, the sword, and the famine,
and the noisome beast, and the
pestilence, to cut off from it man and
beast?*

Ezekiel 33:27 (KJV) Say thou thus unto them, Thus saith the Lord GOD; As I live, surely they that are in the wastes shall fall by the sword, and him that is in the open field will I give to the beasts to be devoured, and they that be in the forts and in the caves shall die of the pestilence

Jeremiah 21:6-9 (KJV) And I will smite the inhabitants of this city, both man and beast: they shall die of a great pestilence.

(7) And afterward, saith the LORD, I will deliver Zedekiah king of Judah, and his servants, and the people, and such as are left in this city from the pestilence, from the sword, and from the famine, into the hand of Nebuchadrezzar king of Babylon, and into the hand of their enemies, and into the hand of those that

seek their life: and he shall smite them with the edge of the sword; he shall not spare them, neither have pity, nor have mercy.

(8) And unto this people thou shalt say, Thus saith the LORD; Behold, I set before you the way of life, and the way of death.

(9) He that abideth in this city shall die by the sword, and by the famine, and by the pestilence: but he that goeth out, and falleth to the Chaldeans that besiege you, he shall live, and his life shall be unto him for a prey.

Revelation 6:8 (KJV) And I looked, and behold a pale horse: and his name that sat on him was Death, and Hell followed with him. And power was given unto them over the fourth part of the earth, to kill with sword, and with

hunger, and with death, and with the
beasts of the earth.

Spiritual meaning

Spiritually, the Plagues represents a
fullness of quantity. The Ten
Egyptian Plagues Means *"Completely*
Plagued". Just as the "Ten
Commandments" became symbolic
of the fullness of the moral law of
God, the ten ancient plagues of
Egypt represent the fullness of God's
expression of justice and judgments,
upon those who oppress and refuse to
repent.

Their purpose

Sometimes in the Bible, plagues are
said to be directly sent by God for a
specific purpose of punishment,
whereas other times they just come

as part of a world where death plays
a part.

But in the land of Egypt however,
the Ten Plagues are the disasters God
sent the Egyptians when Pharaoh
refused to let the Hebrews go free.
The plagues, which are recorded in
the book of Exodus, are a
demonstration of God's power over
not only Pharaoh but also over the
gods of Egypt.

Oppressing the Oppressors

Thousands of years ago, according to
the Old Testament, the Jews were
slaves in Egypt. The Israelites had
been in Egypt for generations, but
now that they had become so
numerous, the Pharaoh feared their
presence.

He feared that one day the Isrealites would turn against the Egyptians. Gradually and stealthily, he forced them to become his slaves. However, the most high God punished these oppressors by unleashing plagues upon the land of Egypt.

The fundamental message is that God brought the plagues on Egypt in order to free the Israelite slaves. God was teaching the ancient Egyptians a lesson about justice, so when they refused to do the right thing and free the Israelites, they suffered the consequences.

Moving on to the next chapter, we shall now discuss the alleged gods of Egypt.

CHAPTER FOUR

Shaming the gods of Egypt

Introduction

*I*n this chapter, we shall discuss elaborately who or what a god is, the conceptual origin, lesser gods like the gods of Egypt, and the one true God, our Father.

What is a god?

A god or deity is a supernatural being considered divine or sacred, or anything revered as divine. It can also be defined as a being with powers greater than those of ordinary humans, but who interacts with humans, positively or negatively, in ways that carry humans to new levels of consciousness, beyond the grounded preoccupations of ordinary life.

So a god can be defined as a superhuman being or spirit worshipped as having power over nature or human fortunes, also known as a deity. The simple definition of a god is an image, person or thing that is worshiped, honored or believed to be all-powerful or the creator and ruler of the universe.

What makes a god a god?

The concept of a god as described by most theologians includes the attributes of omniscience (infinite knowledge), omnipotence (unlimited power), omnipresence (present everywhere), divine simplicity, and as having an eternal and necessary existence.

What they are known for

It's generally believed in several other religions that these gods and goddesses control everything in their lives and the environment. There was technically a god for every aspect of their lives. It was important to please the gods; happy gods helped you, but unhappy gods punished you.

Lesser gods

Put simply, a lesser god could only mean a god relatively smaller than another (comparative). In this context, the word "god" could be used in a figurative meaning, such as

the gods of Egypt are lesser gods in
comparison to the one true God.

The one true God

*Exodus 3:14 (KJV) And God said unto
Moses, I AM THAT I AM: and he
said, Thus shalt thou say unto the
children of Israel, I AM hath sent me
unto you.*

*Exodus 20:2-6 (KJV) (2)I am the
LORD thy God, which have brought
thee out of the land of Egypt, out of the
house of bondage.*
*(3) Thou shalt have no other gods before
me.*
*(4) Thou shalt not make unto thee any
graven image, or any likeness of any
thing that is in heaven above, or that is
in the earth beneath, or that is in the
water under the earth:*

(5) Thou shalt not bow down thyself to them, nor serve them: for I the LORD thy God am a jealous God, visiting the iniquity of the fathers upon the children unto the third and fourth generation of them that hate me;

(6) And shewing mercy unto thousands of them that love me, and keep my commandments.

In monotheistic thought, God is perceived as the supreme being, creator, and principal object of faith. God is usually conceived of as being omnipotent, omniscient, omnipresent and omnibenevolent as well as having an eternal and necessary existence. God is most often held to be incorporeal, with said characteristic being related to conceptions of transcendence or immanence.

Furthermore, the one true God exists in tri-unity. The Bible speaks of three divine Persons who share the same nature and essence in one God. Father, Son, and Holy Spirit are three in one (Matthew 28:19).

Matthew 28:19 (KJV) Go ye therefore, and teach all nations, baptizing them in the name of the Father, and of the Son, and of the Holy Ghost:

This characteristic of the one true God separates Him from all other gods of monotheistic religions: Islam, for example, teaches one god (Allah), but it is a false god, since Allah is not triune. Any concept of God that excludes Jesus Christ is faulty. As Scripture says, *"No one who denies the Son has the Father; whoever*

*acknowledges the Son has the Father
also" (1 John 2:23).*

The gods of Egypt

Ancient Egyptian deities are the gods
and goddesses worshipped in ancient
Egypt. The beliefs and rituals
surrounding these gods formed the
core of ancient Egyptian religion,
which emerged sometime in
prehistory. Deities represented
natural forces and phenomena, and
the Egyptians supported and
appeased them through offerings and
rituals so that these forces would
continue to function according to
maat, or divine order. After the
founding of the Egyptian state
around 3100 BC, the authority to
perform these tasks was controlled by
the pharaoh, who claimed to be the

gods' representative and managed the temples where the rituals were carried out.

So Moses was a great prophet, called by God with a very essential task to do. And as an instrument in the Lord's hand, he performed many signs, or "wonders", attempting to convince Pharaoh to allow the Israelites freedom from their bondage of slavery to the Egyptians. These "wonders" are more commonly referred to as "plagues" sent from the God of Israel, as a proof that the "one true God" was far greater than all of the multiple Gods of the Egyptians, hence, putting these lesser gods to shame. I pray that the Lord will put all your enemies to shame in the mighty name of Jesus, Amen.

CHAPTER FIVE
Shaming Hapi

Introduction

In this chapter, we shall discuss extensively how the Egyptian god Hapi was dishonored by the power of God. We shall also shed light on who this god was and his role in the Egyptian religion.

Who was Hapi?
Hapi (the Nile God) was the god of the annual flooding of the Nile in ancient Egyptian religion. The flood deposited rich silt (fertile soil) on the river's banks, allowing the Egyptians to grow crops. Hapi was greatly celebrated among the Egyptians.

What he was worshipped for

Some of the titles of Hapi were "Lord
of the Fish and Birds of the Marshes"
and "Lord of the River Bringing
Vegetation". Hapi is typically
depicted as an androgynous figure
with a big belly and large drooping
breasts, wearing a loincloth and
ceremonial false beard.

Hapi, in ancient Egyptian religion, is
personification of the annual
inundation of the Nile River. Hapi
was the most important among
numerous personifications of aspects
of natural fertility, and his
dominance increased during
Egyptian history.

The plague

Exodus 7:14-25 (KJV) And the LORD said unto Moses, Pharaoh's heart is hardened, he refuseth to let the people go.

(15) Get thee unto Pharaoh in the morning; lo, he goeth out unto the water; and thou shalt stand by the river's brink against he come; and the rod which was turned to a serpent shalt thou take in thine hand.

(16) And thou shalt say unto him, The LORD God of the Hebrews hath sent me unto thee, saying, Let my people go, that they may serve me in the wilderness: and, behold, hitherto thou wouldest not hear.

(17) Thus saith the LORD, In this thou shalt know that I am the LORD: behold, I will smite with the rod that is in mine hand upon the waters which are

in the river, and they shall be turned to blood.

(18) And the fish that is in the river shall die, and the river shall stink; and the Egyptians shall lothe to drink of the water of the river.

(19) And the LORD spake unto Moses, Say unto Aaron, Take thy rod, and stretch out thine hand upon the waters of Egypt, upon their streams, upon their rivers, and upon their ponds, and upon all their pools of water, that they may become blood; and that there may be blood throughout all the land of Egypt, both in vessels of wood, and in vessels of stone.

(20) And Moses and Aaron did so, as the LORD commanded; and he lifted up the rod, and smote the waters that were in the river, in the sight of Pharaoh, and in the sight of his servants; and all

the waters that were in the river were turned to blood.

(21) And the fish that was in the river died; and the river stank, and the Egyptians could not drink of the water of the river; and there was blood throughout all the land of Egypt.

(22) And the magicians of Egypt did so with their enchantments: and Pharaoh's heart was hardened, neither did he hearken unto them; as the LORD had said.

(23) And Pharaoh turned and went into his house, neither did he set his heart to this also.

(24) And all the Egyptians digged round about the river for water to drink; for they could not drink of the water of the river.

(25) And seven days were fulfilled, after that the LORD had smitten the river.

The first plague that was given to the Egyptians from God was that of turning the Nile river to blood. As Aaron, the spokesman for Moses, touched the "rod" of the Lord to the Nile River, it immediately turned to blood, all the fish died, and the river stank.

Partially able to duplicate this miracle, the magicians of Pharaoh also turn water into blood, leaving Pharaoh unimpressed with this great wonder from God.

However, for seven days the water throughout all the land of Egypt remained in this state, and it was obviously unsuitable for drinking, the perfect length of time to demonstrate that the Lord was superior to all the other Gods of Egypt, especially Hapi, thus putting that god to shame.

CHAPTER SIX

Shaming Heket

Introduction

In this chapter, we shall discuss extensively how the Egyptian goddess Heket was dishonored by the power of God. We shall also shed light on who this goddess was and her role in the Egyptian religion.

Who was Heket?

Heqet, sometimes spelled Heket, is an Egyptian goddess of fertility, water and renewal, often identified with Hathor, and represented in the form of a frog.

To the Egyptians, the frog was an ancient symbol of fertility, related to the annual flooding of the Nile.

Heqet was originally the female counterpart of Khnum, or the wife of Khnum by whom she became the mother of Her-ur. It has been proposed that her name is the origin of the name of Hecate, the Greek goddess of witchcraft.

What she was worshipped for

The worship of the frog was one of the oldest cults in Egypt. Frog gods and frog goddesses were thought to have had a vital role in the creation of the world. Just prior to the annual flooding of the Nile River, frogs would appear in great numbers, possibly leading to their association with fecundity and with the beginning of life in the world.

The plague

Exodus 8:1-15 (KJV) And the LORD spake unto Moses, Go unto Pharaoh, and say unto him, Thus saith the LORD, Let my people go, that they may serve me.

(2) And if thou refuse to let them go, behold, I will smite all thy borders with frogs:

(3) And the river shall bring forth frogs abundantly, which shall go up and come into thine house, and into thy bedchamber, and upon thy bed, and into the house of thy servants, and upon thy people, and into thine ovens, and into thy kneadingtroughs:

(4) And the frogs shall come up both on thee, and upon thy people, and upon all thy servants.

(5) And the LORD spake unto Moses, Say unto Aaron, Stretch forth thine hand with thy rod over the streams, over the rivers, and over the ponds, and cause frogs to come up upon the land of Egypt.

(6) And Aaron stretched out his hand over the waters of Egypt; and the frogs came up, and covered the land of Egypt.

(7) And the magicians did so with their enchantments, and brought up frogs upon the land of Egypt.

(8) Then Pharaoh called for Moses and Aaron, and said, Intreat the LORD, that he may take away the frogs from me, and from my people; and I will let the people go, that they may do sacrifice unto the LORD.

(9) And Moses said unto Pharaoh, Glory over me: when shall I intreat for thee, and for thy servants, and for thy people, to destroy the frogs from thee and thy houses, that they may remain in the river only?

(10) And he said, To morrow. And he said, Be it according to thy word: that thou mayest know that there is none like unto the LORD our God.

(11) And the frogs shall depart from thee, and from thy houses, and from thy servants, and from thy people; they shall remain in the river only.

(12) And Moses and Aaron went out from Pharaoh: and Moses cried unto the LORD because of the frogs which he had brought against Pharaoh.

(13) And the LORD did according to the word of Moses; and the frogs died

out of the houses, out of the villages, and out of the fields.
(14) And they gathered them together upon heaps: and the land stank.
(15) But when Pharaoh saw that there was respite, he hardened his heart, and hearkened not unto them; as the LORD had said.

Still, Pharaoh refused to let the children of Israel go from the presence of Egypt. The second plague that was extended upon Egypt, from the "rod" by Aaron, was that of frogs.

The frogs came up from the river and were in their houses, in their food, in their clothing, in every place possible. From the greatest to the least, no one in Egypt escaped the plague of frogs. Pharaoh's magicians were able to bring more frogs in their attempt to imitate the power of God, but only Moses was able to make the frogs go away. This was another disgrace on a famous Egyptian Goddess, Heket.

CHAPTER SEVEN

Shaming Geb

Introduction

In this chapter, we shall discuss extensively how the Egyptian god Geb was dishonored by the power of God. We shall also shed light on who this god was and his role in the Egyptian religion.

Who was Geb?

Geb was the Egyptian god of the earth and a mythological member of the Ennead of Heliopolis. He could also be considered a father of snakes. It was believed in ancient Egypt that

Geb's laughter created earthquakes and that he allowed crops to grow.

What he was worshipped for

Thousands of years ago, Geb was worshipped in lower Egypt as the earth god. Geb was depicted as a bearded man with a goose on his head. He was the provider of crops and a healer. Egyptian people believed that Geb's laughter caused earthquakes.

Furthermore, Egyptologists have found temples dedicated to Geb in several areas of Egypt. Heliopolis was the center of Geb's worship though and the priests there considered Geb the father of the sun. They believed that he and Nut laid the cosmic egg that contained the sun.

The plague

Exodus 8:16-19 (KJV) And the LORD said unto Moses, Say unto Aaron, Stretch out thy rod, and smite the dust of the land, that it may become lice throughout all the land of Egypt.

(17) And they did so; for Aaron stretched out his hand with his rod, and smote the dust of the earth, and it became lice in man, and in beast; all the dust of the land became lice throughout all the land of Egypt.

(18) And the magicians did so with their enchantments to bring forth lice, but they could not: so there were lice upon man, and upon beast.

(19) Then the magicians said unto Pharaoh, This is the finger of God: and Pharaoh's heart was hardened, and he hearkened not unto them; as the LORD had said.

Still Pharaoh would not concede, even after this display of power from the Lord, or magnificent plague, he still would not let them go. So at the command of the Lord to Moses, Aaron was told to stretch forth his rod and smite the dust of the earth. When he did, the dust became lice throughout all the land, on both people and beasts. The very dust that was referred to in the creation process of man is now used to plague men, as a reminder of his mortality and sin which both lead to death.

Finally, the magicians of Pharaoh and Geb were humiliated, being unable to compete with this power that was so far greater than themselves and the powers that they had from their Egyptian gods and

goddesses, and they professed, "this is
the finger of God."

This was the last plague that required
Aaron's involvement, as the next set
of three plagues are issued by the
word of Moses himself. Let's look
into them.

CHAPTER EIGHT

Shaming Khepri

Introduction

In this chapter, we shall discuss extensively how the Egyptian god Khepri was dishonored by the power of God. We shall also shed light on who this god was and his role in the Egyptian religion.

Who was Khepri?

Khepri (Egyptian: ḥprj, also transliterated Khepera, Kheper, Khepra and Chepri) was a scarab-faced god in ancient Egyptian religion who represented the rising or morning sun. By extension, he also represented creation and the renewal of life.

What he was worshipped for

As a deity, Khepri was worshipped
for his four main functions were
creation, protection, sun-god, and
the god of resurrection. The central
belief surrounding Khepri was the
god's ability to renew life, in the
same way he restored the sun's
existence every morning.

The plague

*Exodus 8:20-32 (KJV) And the
LORD said unto Moses, Rise up early
in the morning, and stand before
Pharaoh; lo, he cometh forth to the
water; and say unto him, Thus saith the
LORD, Let my people go, that they
may serve me.*

*(21) Else, if thou wilt not let my people
go, behold, I will send swarms of flies*

*upon thee, and upon thy servants, and
upon thy people, and into thy houses:
and the houses of the Egyptians shall be
full of swarms of flies, and also the
ground whereon they are.*

*(22) And I will sever in that day the
land of Goshen, in which my people
dwell, that no swarms of flies shall be
there; to the end thou mayest know that
I am the LORD in the midst of the
earth.*

*(23) And I will put a division between
my people and thy people: to morrow
shall this sign be.*

*(24) And the LORD did so; and there
came a grievous swarm of flies into the
house of Pharaoh, and into his servants'
houses, and into all the land of Egypt:
the land was corrupted by reason of the
swarm of flies.*

(25) And Pharaoh called for Moses and for Aaron, and said, Go ye, sacrifice to your God in the land.

(26) And Moses said, It is not meet so to do; for we shall sacrifice the abomination of the Egyptians to the LORD our God: lo, shall we sacrifice the abomination of the Egyptians before their eyes, and will they not stone us?

(27) We will go three days' journey into the wilderness, and sacrifice to the LORD our God, as he shall command us.

(28) And Pharaoh said, I will let you go, that ye may sacrifice to the LORD your God in the wilderness; only ye shall not go very far away: intreat for me.

(29) And Moses said, Behold, I go out from thee, and I will intreat the LORD that the swarms of flies may depart from

*Pharaoh, from his servants, and from his
people, tomorrow: but let not Pharaoh
deal deceitfully any more in not letting
the people go to sacrifice to the LORD.*

*(30) And Moses went out from
Pharaoh, and intreated the LORD.*

*(31) And the LORD did according to
the word of Moses; and he removed the
swarms of flies from Pharaoh, from his
servants, and from his people; there
remained not one.*

*(32) And Pharaoh hardened his heart at
this time also, neither would he let the
people go.*

With the fourth Egyptian plague,
which consisted of flies, begins the
great miracle of separation or
differentiation.

Moses met Pharaoh at the Nile River in the morning and made the demand, speaking on behalf of the Lord, "Let My peole go, that they may serve Me." Again, Pharaoh hardened his heart and disregarded the request, resulting in a pronouncement of swarms of flies.

This time however, only the Egyptians were affected by the judgement, or plague, and the children of Israel remain unharmed.

This wonder also elevated the Egyptian plagues to a different level, adding destruction as well as discomfort to the consequence of their decisions.

Plagued by flies, Pharaoh tried a new tactic bargained with the Lord, showing his desire to maintain power and authority over God. He tried to dictate the terms and conditions of the offer, telling them they may sacrifice but only "in the land" clearly not complying with the requested "three days' journey" that the Lord required.

This temporary allowance is made solely to have Moses "intreat the Lord that the swarms of flies may depart", at this point Pharaoh has learned in part who the Lord is and asks for His assistance over the Egyptian gods and goddesses, clearly revealing the Lord's dominance over Khepri and these lesser gods.

However, as soon as the request is granted by the Lord, Pharaoh reneges on his promise and will not let them go, and continues to worship his Egyptian Gods.

CHAPTER NINE

Shaming Hathor

Introduction

In this chapter, we shall discuss extensively how the Egyptian goddess Hathor was dishonored by the power of God. We shall also shed light on who this goddess was and her role in the Egyptian religion.

Who was Hathor?

Hathor, in ancient Egyptian religion, was the goddess of the sky, of women, and of fertility and love. Hathor's worship originated in early dynastic times (3rd millennium BCE).

The name Hathor means "estate or house of Horus" and this may not even have been her original name. Her principal animal form was that of a cow, and she was strongly associated with motherhood. Hathor was closely connected with the sun god Re of Heliopolis, whose "eye" or daughter she was said to be. In her cult centre at Dandarah in Upper Egypt, she was worshipped with Horus.

What she was worshipped for?

Hathor was a famous ancient goddess, highly loved and worshipped throughout Egypt, starting from the 3rd millennium BCE. She was the goddess of motherhood, love, joy, fertility, dance, and beauty.

During the New Kingdom however, which lasted between 1550–1070 BC, goddesses such as Mut and Isis encroached on Hathor's position in royal ideology, but she remained one of the most widely worshipped deities. After the end of the New Kingdom, Hathor was increasingly overshadowed by Isis, but she continued to be venerated until the extinction of ancient Egyptian religion in the early centuries AD.

The plague

Exodus 9:1-7 (KJV) Then the LORD said unto Moses, Go in unto Pharaoh, and tell him, Thus saith the LORD God of the Hebrews, Let my people go, that they may serve me.
(2) For if thou refuse to let them go, and wilt hold them still,

(3) Behold, the hand of the LORD is upon thy cattle which is in the field, upon the horses, upon the asses, upon the camels, upon the oxen, and upon the sheep: there shall be a very grievous murrain.

(4) And the LORD shall sever between the cattle of Israel and the cattle of Egypt: and there shall nothing die of all that is the children of Israel.

(5) And the LORD appointed a set time, saying, ``Tomorrow the LORD shall do this thing in the land.

(6) And the LORD did that thing on the morrow, and all the cattle of Egypt died: but of the cattle of the children of Israel died not one.

(7) And Pharaoh sent, and, behold, there was not one of the cattle of the Israelites

dead. And the heart of Pharaoh was hardened, and he did not let the people go.

Moses once again demanded of Pharaoh, "Let my people go, that they may serve me", revealing also the next Egyptian plague to occur on the condition of continued disobedience to the request.

This plague was given with an advanced warning, allowing a period of repentance to occur, which clearly was not obeyed.

"Tomorrow" the hand of the Lord would be felt upon all the cattle and livestock, of only the Egyptians, as "grievous murrain."

This means that sickness and pestilence would fall upon their livestock with so severe a consequence as to cause them to perish.

This plague affected the Egyptian by creating a huge economic disaster, in areas of food, transportation, military supplies, farming, and economic goods that were produced by these livestock. Still Pharaoh's heart remained hard and he would not listen to the Lord but remained faith to the Egyptian gods and goddesses, the same deity our Lord thoroughly put to shame.

CHAPTER TEN

Shaming Isis

Introduction

In this chapter, we shall discuss extensively how the Egyptian goddess Isis was dishonored by the power of God. We shall also shed light on who this goddess was and her role in the Egyptian religion.

Who was Isis?

Isis was a goddess in Egyptian mythology. She was known as the goddess of the moon. As goddess of life and magic, Isis protected women and children, and healed the sick. Closely linked to the throne, she was one of the greatest goddesses of Ancient Egypt.

What she was worshipped for?

Isis was a major goddess in ancient Egyptian religion whose worship spread throughout the Greco-Roman world. In the first millennium BCE, Osiris and Isis became the most widely worshipped Egyptian deities, and Isis absorbed traits from many other goddesses. Rulers in Egypt and its neighbor to the south, Nubia, built temples dedicated primarily to Isis, and her temple at Philae was a religious center for Egyptians and Nubians alike.

Her reputed magical power was allegedly greater than that of all other gods, and she was said to protect the kingdom from its enemies, govern the skies and the natural world, and have power over fate itself.

The plague

Exodus 9:8-12 (KJV) And the LORD said unto Moses and unto Aaron, Take to you handfuls of ashes of the furnace, and let Moses sprinkle it toward heaven in the sight of Pharaoh.

(9) And it shall become small dust in all the land of Egypt, and shall be a boil breaking forth with blains upon man, and upon beast, throughout all the land of Egypt.

(10) And they took ashes of the furnace, and stood before Pharaoh; and Moses sprinkled it up toward heaven; and it

*became a boil breaking forth with blains
upon man, and upon beast. (11) And the
magicians could not stand before Moses
because of the boils; for the boil was
upon the magicians, and upon all the
Egyptians.*

*(12) And the LORD hardened the heart
of Pharaoh, and he hearkened not unto
them; as the LORD had spoken unto
Moses.*

Unannounced the sixth Egyptian
plague is given, for the first time,
directly attacking the Egyptian
people themselves. Being instructed
by the Lord, Moses took ashes from
the furnace of affliction, and threw
them into the air. As the dust from
the ashes blew all over Egypt, it
settled on man and beast alike in the
form   of   boils   and   sores.

As with the previous two, throughout the remaining Egyptian plagues the division is drawn between the Egyptians and the children of Israel, as God gives protection to his covenant people.

The severity of the judgment of God has now become personal, as it is actually felt by the people themselves. Cleanliness being paramount in Egyptian society, this plague pronounces the people "unclean."

The so-called magicians who have been seen throughout the previous plagues are unable to perform ceremonially rituals to their Egyptian gods and goddesses in this unclean state, not allowing them to even stand before Pharaoh; its observed that they are no longer referred to in the scriptures. Once again, a lesser Egyptian goddess has been shamed by the "One True God"

CHAPTER ELEVEN

Shaming Nut

Introduction

In this chapter, we shall discuss extensively how the Egyptian goddess Nut was dishonored by the power of God. We shall also shed light on who this goddess was and her role in the Egyptian religion.

Who was Nut?

According to ancient Egyptian mythology, Nut (pronounced "newt") is the goddess of the sky and heavens. She was the daughter of Shu, god of vital breath, and his wife Tefnut, goddess of heat.

She was usually depicted as a woman bent over Earth with her head in the West and feet in the East.

What she was worshipped for

Although Nut was important to the ancient Egyptians, she was seldom worshipped in the same way as many other gods and is not very well-known in modern times, except to those who study ancient Egyptian culture. However, Nut represented many things to ancient Egyptians. She was a protector and provider, often depicted as a cow—a symbol of nourishment.

The plague

*Exodus 9:13-35 (KJV) And the
LORD said unto Moses, Rise up early
in the morning, and stand before
Pharaoh, and say unto him, Thus saith
the LORD God of the Hebrews, Let my
people go, that they may serve me.*

*(14) For I will at this time send all my
plagues upon thine heart, and upon thy
servants, and upon thy people; that thou
mayest know that there is none like me
in all the earth.*

*(15) For now I will stretch out my hand,
that I may smite thee and thy people
with pestilence; and thou shalt be cut off
from the earth.*

*(16) And in every deed for this cause
have I raised thee up, for to shew in thee
my power; and that my name may be
declared throughout all the earth.*

(17) As yet exaltest thou thyself against my people, that thou wilt not let them go?

(18) Behold, tomorrow about this time I will cause it to rain a very grievous hail, such as hath not been in Egypt since the foundation thereof even until now.

(19) Send therefore now, and gather thy cattle, and all that thou hast in the field; for upon every man and beast which shall be found in the field, and shall not be brought home, the hail shall come down upon them, and they shall die.

(20) He that feared the word of the LORD among the servants of Pharaoh made his servants and his cattle flee into the houses:

(21) And he that regarded not the word of the LORD left his servants and his cattle in the field.

*(22) And the LORD said unto Moses,
Stretch forth thine hand toward heaven,
that there may be hail in all the land of
Egypt, upon man, and upon beast, and
upon every herb of the field, throughout
the land of Egypt.*

*(23) And Moses stretched forth his rod
toward heaven: and the LORD sent
thunder and hail, and the fire ran along
upon the ground; and the LORD rained
hail upon the land of Egypt.*

*(24) So there was hail, and fire mingled
with the hail, very grievous, such as there
was none like it in all the land of Egypt
since it became a nation.*

*(25) And the hail smote throughout all
the land of Egypt all that was in the
field, both man and beast; and the hail
smote every herb of the field, and brake
every tree of the field.*

(26) Only in the land of Goshen, where the children of Israel were, was there no hail.

(27) And Pharaoh sent, and called for Moses and Aaron, and said unto them, I have sinned this time: the LORD is righteous, and I and my people are wicked.

(28) Intreat the LORD (for it is enough) that there be no more mighty thunderings and hail; and I will let you go, and ye shall stay no longer.

(29) And Moses said unto him, As soon as I am gone out of the city, I will spread abroad my hands unto the LORD; and the thunder shall cease, neither shall there be any more hail; that thou mayest know how that the earth is the LORD'S.

(30) But as for thee and thy servants, I know that ye will not yet fear the LORD God.

(31) And the flax and the barley was smitten: for the barley was in the ear, and the flax was bolled.

(32) But the wheat and the rie were not smitten: for they were not grown up.

(33) And Moses went out of the city from Pharaoh, and spread abroad his hands unto the LORD: and the thunders and hail ceased, and the rain was not poured upon the earth.

(34) And when Pharaoh saw that the rain and the hail and the thunders were ceased, he sinned yet more, and hardened his heart, he and his servants.

(35) And the heart of Pharaoh was hardened, neither would he let the children of Israel go; as the LORD had spoken by Moses.

Again warning is given before the enactment of the plague takes place. Pharaoh is warned of the impending doom that will be faced if he does not listen to the Lord, and forget his own Egyptian gods and goddesses. Hail of unspeakable size and ability to destroy, would rain down from the sky and turn to fire as it hit the ground. The Lord, in showing Pharaoh that "there is none like Him in the Earth", allows those who are willing to hear His word, and do as He commands, to be saved.

A division is now felt between the Egyptians in the form of those "converted" to the Lord, as shown by their obedience and willingness to escape to the protection of their "houses."

Similarly, we are warned to make our houses a place of refuge from the world today. Interestingly enough, the crops that were destroyed by the hail consisted of flax and barley, which were ripening in the fields.

These two particular crops were not the mainstay of their diet, but were used more specifically for their clothing and libations.

This destruction would make their life uncomfortable, but as far as affecting their food supply, the wheat still survived. This gave the Egyptians still another chance to turn to "the One True God", and forsake their own Egyptian gods and goddesses, thus showing God's mercy and grace even yet.

CHAPTER TWELVE

Shaming Seth

Introduction

In this chapter, we shall discuss
extensively how the Egyptian god
Seth was dishonored by the power of
God. We shall also shed light on who
this god was and his role in the
Egyptian religion.

Who was Seth?

Seth (Set), son of Geb (Earth) and
Nut (sky), brother of Osiris, was god
of the desert, foreign lands,
thunderstorms, eclipses, and
earthquakes. Seth was a powerful and
often frightening deity, however he
was also a patron god of the

pharaohs, particularly Ramses the Great.

What he was worshipped for

Seth was the ancient Egyptian god of chaos and represented everything that threatened harmony in the land of Egypt. It's believed that at first, Egyptians prayed and worshipped Seth so that he would take care of the dead family members, but over time he became seen as much more evil.

During the rule of the Hyksos invaders between 1630–1521, Seth was worshipped at their capital, Avaris, in the northeastern Nile River delta, and was identified with the Canaanite storm god Baal.

During the New Kingdom era which lasted between 1539–c. 1075 bce, Seth was worshipped as a martial god who could sow discord among Egypt's enemies.

The plague

Exodus 10:1-20 (KJV) And the LORD said unto Moses, Go in unto Pharaoh: for I have hardened his heart, and the heart of his servants, that I might shew these my signs before him:

(2) And that thou mayest tell in the ears of thy son, and of thy son's son, what things I have wrought in Egypt, and my signs which I have done among them; that ye may know how that I am the LORD. (3) And Moses and Aaron came in unto Pharaoh, and said unto him, Thus saith the LORD God of the Hebrews, How long wilt thou refuse to

humble thyself before me? let my people go, that they may serve me.

(4) Else, if thou refuse to let my people go, behold, tomorrow will I bring the locusts into thy coast:

(5) And they shall cover the face of the earth, that one cannot be able to see the earth: and they shall eat the residue of that which is escaped, which remaineth unto you from the hail, and shall eat every tree which groweth for you out of the field:

(6) And they shall fill thy houses, and the houses of all thy servants, and the houses of all the Egyptians; which neither thy fathers, nor thy fathers' fathers have seen, since the day that they were upon the earth unto this day. And he turned himself, and went out from Pharaoh.

(7) And Pharaoh's servants said unto him, How long shall this man be a snare unto us? let the men go, that they may serve the LORD their God: knowest thou not yet that Egypt is destroyed?

(8) And Moses and Aaron were brought again unto Pharaoh: and he said unto them, Go, serve the LORD your God: but who are they that shall go?

(9) And Moses said, We will go with our young and with our old, with our sons and with our daughters, with our flocks and with our herds will we go; for we must hold a feast unto the LORD.

(10) And he said unto them, Let the LORD be so with you, as I will let you go, and your little ones: look to it; for evil is before you.

(11) Not so: go now ye that are men, and serve the LORD; for that ye did

desire. And they were driven out from Pharaoh's presence.

(12) And the LORD said unto Moses, Stretch out thine hand over the land of Egypt for the locusts, that they may come up upon the land of Egypt, and eat every herb of the land, even all that the hail hath left.

(13) And Moses stretched forth his rod over the land of Egypt, and the LORD brought an east wind upon the land all that day, and all that night; and when it was morning, the east wind brought the locusts.

(14) And the locusts went up over all the land of Egypt, and rested in all the coasts of Egypt: very grievous were they; before them there were no such locusts as they, neither after them shall be such.

(15) For they covered the face of the whole earth, so that the land was

darkened; and they did eat every herb of the land, and all the fruit of the trees which the hail had left: and there remained not any green thing in the trees, or in the herbs of the field, through all the land of Egypt.

(16) Then Pharaoh called for Moses and Aaron in haste; and he said, I have sinned against the LORD your God, and against you.

(17) Now therefore forgive, I pray thee, my sin only this once, and intreat the LORD your God, that he may take away from me this death only.

(18) And he went out from Pharaoh, and intreated the LORD.

(19) And the LORD turned a mighty strong west wind, which took away the locusts, and cast them into the Red sea; there remained not one locust in all the coasts of Egypt.

(20) But the LORD hardened Pharaoh's heart, so that he would not let the children of Israel go.

Still Pharaoh would not listen to the message of the Lord, still he relies on his own Egyptian gods and goddesses. The eighth plague issued by the Lord had an even greater purpose than all the others, it was to be felt so that Pharaoh would tell even "his sons and son's sons" the mighty things of the Lord, thus teaching even future generations of the power of the "strong hand of God" over all the other Egyptian gods and goddesses.

Moses and Aaron approached
Pharaoh with the same request, "Let
my people go so that they may serve
me", and pronounced the judgment
of locusts if not heeded. This is the
second wave of destruction to follow
the hail, and whatever crops were left
intact after that display, were now
completely consumed by the swarms
of locusts that were unleashed from
the sky.

This wonder definitely affected their
life source. By hitting them in their
food supply, the Lord displayed the
possibility of imminent death if a
change of heart did not occur. Yet
still, Pharaoh would not listen.

CHAPTER THIRTEEN

Shaming Ra

Introduction

In this chapter, we shall discuss extensively how the Egyptian god Ra was dishonored by the power of God. We shall also shed light on who this god was and his role in the Egyptian religion.

Who was Ra?

Amun-Ra, Ra, Rah or Re, was the ancient Egyptian deity of the sun. By the Fifth Dynasty in the 25th and 24th centuries BC, he had become one of the most important gods in ancient Egyptian religion, identified primarily with the noon sun.

Ra was believed to rule in all parts of
the created world: the sky, the Earth,
and the underworld. He was the god
of the sun, order, kings and the sky.

What he was worshipped for

Because of the life-giving qualities of
the sun the Egyptians worshiped the
sun as a god. The creator of the
universe and the giver of life, the sun
or Ra represented life, warmth and
growth.

Amun-Ra was the chief of the
Egyptian gods. In the early days of
the Egyptian civilization, he was
worshipped as two separate gods.
Amun was the god who created the
universe. Ra was the god of the sun
and light, who traveled across the sky
every day in a burning boat.

The plague

Exodus 10:21-29 (KJV) And the LORD said unto Moses, Stretch out thine hand toward heaven, that there may be darkness over the land of Egypt, even darkness which may be felt.

(22) And Moses stretched forth his hand toward heaven; and there was a thick darkness in all the land of Egypt three days:

(23) They saw not one another, neither rose any from his place for three days: but all the children of Israel had light in their dwellings.

(24) And Pharaoh called unto Moses, and said, Go ye, serve the LORD; only let your flocks and your herds be stayed: let your little ones also go with you.

(25) And Moses said, Thou must give us also sacrifices and burnt offerings,

*that we may sacrifice unto the LORD
our God.*

*(26) Our cattle also shall go with us;
there shall not an hoof be left behind; for
thereof must we take to serve the LORD
our God; and we know not with what
we must serve the LORD, until we
come thither.*

*(27) But the LORD hardened
Pharaoh's heart, and he would not let
them go.*

*(28) And Pharaoh said unto him, Get
thee from me, take heed to thyself, see
my face no more; for in that day thou
seest my face thou shalt die.*

*(29) And Moses said, Thou hast spoken
well, I will see thy face again no more.*

Darkness now fell upon Egypt,
unannounced, as a prelude to the
future fate to be felt by the Egyptian
empire when the message of the

Lord was not heeded, and they still turned to their own Egyptian gods and goddesses.

Three days of palpable darkness, that was so immense it could be physically felt, covered the land of Egypt.
The sun, the most worshipped God in Egypt other than Pharaoh himself, gave no light. The Lord showed that he had control over the sun as a witness that the God of Israel had ultimate power over life and death.

The psychological and religious impact would have had a profound influence on the Egyptians at this point. Darkness was a representation of death, judgment and hopelessness. Darkness was a complete absence of light.

CHAPTER FOURTEEN

Shaming Pharaoh – Osiris and Horus

Introduction

We shall now discuss who the ruler of ancient Egypt titled Pharaoh really is along with its deific symbolism. We shall also shed light on the one plague that finally broke the Pharaoh's hardened heart; The Angel of Death.

What is a Pharaoh?

The word "pharaoh" means "Great House," a reference to the palace where the pharaoh resides. While early Egyptian rulers were called "kings," over time, the name "pharaoh" remained.

The Pharaohs of Ancient Egypt were the supreme leaders of the land. They were like kings or emperors. They ruled both upper and lower Egypt and were both the political and religious leaders. The Pharaoh was often thought of as one of the gods.

Its deific symbolism

The Egyptians believed their pharaoh to be the mediator between the gods and the world of men. After death the pharaoh became divine, identified with Osiris, the father of Horus and god of the dead, and passed on his sacred powers and position to the new pharaoh, his son.

The Ancient Egyptians believed that their Pharaoh was the god Horus, son of Re, the sun god. When a pharaoh died he was believed to be united with the sun and then a new Horus ruled on earth.

As a divine ruler, the pharaoh was the preserver of the god-given order, called maat. He owned a large portion of Egypt's land and directed its use, was responsible for his people's economic and spiritual welfare, and dispensed justice to his subjects.

The Angel of Death

Exodus 11:1-10 (KJV) And the LORD said unto Moses, Yet will I bring one plague more upon Pharaoh, and upon Egypt; afterwards he will let you go hence: when he shall let you go, he shall surely thrust you out hence altogether.

(2) Speak now in the ears of the people, and let every man borrow of his neighbour, and every woman of her neighbour, jewels of silver, and jewels of gold.

(3) And the LORD gave the people favour in the sight of the Egyptians. Moreover the man. Moses was very great in the land of Egypt, in the sight of Pharaoh's servants, and in the sight of the people.

*(4) And Moses said, Thus saith the
LORD, About midnight will I go out
into the midst of Egypt:*
*(5) And all the firstborn in the land of
Egypt shall die, from the firstborn of
Pharaoh that sitteth upon his throne,
even unto the firstborn of the
maidservant that is behind the mill; and
all the firstborn of beasts.*
*(6) And there shall be a great cry
throughout all the land of Egypt, such as
there was none like it, nor shall be like
it any more.*
*(7) But against any of the children of
Israel shall not a dog move his tongue,
against man or beast: that ye may know
how that the LORD doth put a
difference between the Egyptians and
Israel.*
*(8) And all these thy servants shall come
down unto me, and bow down*

themselves unto me, saying, Get thee out, and all the people that follow thee: and after that I will go out. And he went out from Pharaoh in a great anger.

(9) And the LORD said unto Moses, Pharaoh shall not hearken unto you; that my wonders may be multiplied in the land of Egypt.

(10) And Moses and Aaron did all these wonders before Pharaoh: and the LORD hardened Pharaoh's heart, so that he would not let the children of Israel go out of his land.

Exodus 12:1-30 (KJV) And the LORD spake unto Moses and Aaron in the land of Egypt, saying,

(2) This month shall be unto you the beginning of months: it shall be the first month of the year to you.

(3) Speak ye unto all the congregation of Israel, saying, In the tenth day of this month they shall take to them every man a lamb, according to the house of their fathers, a lamb for an house:

(4) And if the household be too little for the lamb, let him and his neighbour next unto his house take it according to the number of the souls; every man according to his eating shall make your count for the lamb.

(5) Your lamb shall be without blemish, a male of the first year: ye shall take it out from the sheep, or from the goats:

(6) And ye shall keep it up until the fourteenth day of the same month: and the whole assembly of the congregation of Israel shall kill it in the evening.

(7) And they shall take of the blood, and strike it on the two side posts and on the

upper door post of the houses, wherein they shall eat it.

(8) And they shall eat the flesh in that night, roast with fire, and unleavened bread; and with bitter herbs they shall eat it.

(9) Eat not of it raw, nor sodden at all with water, but roast with fire; his head with his legs, and with the purtenance thereof.

(10) And ye shall let nothing of it remain until the morning; and that which remaineth of it until the morning ye shall burn with fire.

(11) And thus shall ye eat it; with your loins girded, your shoes on your feet, and your staff in your hand; and ye shall eat it in haste: it is the LORD'S passover.

(12) For I will pass through the land of Egypt this night, and will smite all the firstborn in the land of Egypt, both man

*and beast; and against all the gods of
Egypt I will execute judgment: I am the
LORD.*

*(13) And the blood shall be to you for a
token upon the houses where ye are: and
when I see the blood, I will pass over
you, and the plague shall not be upon
you to destroy you, when I smite the
land of Egypt.*

*(14) And this day shall be unto you for
a memorial; and ye shall keep it a feast
to the LORD throughout your
generations; ye shall keep it a feast by
an ordinance for ever.*

*(15) Seven days shall ye eat unleavened
bread; even the first day ye shall put
away leaven out of your houses: for
whosoever eateth leavened bread from
the first day until the seventh day, that
soul shall be cut off from Israel.*

(16) And in the first day there shall be an holy convocation, and in the seventh day there shall be an holy convocation to you; no manner of work shall be done in them, save that which every man must eat, that only may be done of you.

(17) And ye shall observe the feast of unleavened bread; for in this selfsame day have I brought your armies out of the land of Egypt: therefore shall ye observe this day in your generations by an ordinance forever.

(18) In the first month, on the fourteenth day of the month at even, ye shall eat unleavened bread, until the one and twentieth day of the month at even.

(19) Seven days shall there be no leaven found in your houses: for whosoever eateth that which is leavened, even that soul shall be cut off from the

congregation of Israel, whether he be a stranger, or born in the land.

(20) Ye shall eat nothing leavened; in all your habitations shall ye eat unleavened bread.

(21) Then Moses called for all the elders of Israel, and said unto them, Draw out and take you a lamb according to your families, and kill the passover.

(22) And ye shall take a bunch of hyssop, and dip it in the blood that is in the bason, and strike the lintel and the two side posts with the blood that is in the bason; and none of you shall go out at the door of his house until the morning.

(23) For the LORD will pass through to smite the Egyptians; and when he seeth the blood upon the lintel, and on the two side posts, the LORD will pass over the door, and will not suffer the

*destroyer to come in unto your houses to
smite you.*

*(24) And ye shall observe this thing for
an ordinance to thee and to thy sons
forever.*

*(25) And it shall come to pass, when ye
be come to the land which the LORD
will give you, according as he hath
promised, that ye shall keep this service.*

*(26) And it shall come to pass, when
your children shall say unto you, What
mean ye by this service?*

*(27) That ye shall say, It is the sacrifice
of the LORD'S passover, who passed
over the houses of the children of Israel
in Egypt, when he smote the Egyptians,
and delivered our houses. And the
people bowed the head and worshipped.*

*(28) And the children of Israel went
away, and did as the LORD had*

commanded Moses and Aaron, so did they.

(29) And it came to pass, that at midnight the LORD smote all the firstborn in the land of Egypt, from the firstborn of Pharaoh that sat on his throne unto the firstborn of the captive that was in the dungeon; and all the firstborn of cattle.

(30) And Pharaoh rose up in the night, he, and all his servants, and all the Egyptians; and there was a great cry in Egypt; for there was not a house where there was not one dead.

In the Hebrew Bible, the destroying angel, also known as mashḥit, is an entity sent out by Yahweh on several occasions to kill the enemies of the Hebrews.

These angels (mal'akh) are also variously referred to as executioners, slayers or Angel of the Lord. The latter is found in Job 33:22, as well as in Proverbs 16:14 in the plural, "messengers of death".

Job 33:22 (KJV) Yea, his soul draweth near unto the grave, and his life to the destroyers.
Proverbs 16:14 The wrath of a king is as messengers of death: but a wise man will pacify it.

Let my people go

Pharaoh, the king of Egypt, was worshipped by the Egyptians because he was considered to be the greatest Egyptian God of all. It was believed that he was actually the son of Ra himself, manifest in the flesh.

After the plague of darkness felt throughout the land was lifted, Pharaoh resumed his position of "bargaining with the Lord" and offered Moses another "deal." Since virtually all of the Egyptian animals had been consumed by the judgments of the Lord, Pharaoh now consented to the request made, to let the people go, but they must leave their animals in Egypt

This was a totally unacceptable offer, as the animals were to be used as the actual sacrifice to the Lord.

The Lord is uncompromising when He has set the terms. Enraged by the refusal, Pharaoh pronounced the last deadly plague to be unleashed upon the land from his very own lips as he warns Moses, "Get thee from me, take heed to thyself, see my face no more; for in that day thou seest my face thou shalt die."

The Passover Feast

The Passover Feast commemorates Israel's deliverance from slavery in Egypt. On Passover, Jews also celebrate the birth of the Jewish nation after being freed by God from captivity.

Today, the Jewish people not only celebrate Passover as a historical event but in a broader sense, celebrate their freedom as Jews.

During Passover, Jews take part in the Seder meal, which incorporates the retelling of Exodus and God's deliverance from bondage in Egypt. Each participant of the Seder experiences in a personal way, a national celebration of freedom through God's intervention and deliverance.

In Exodus 12, a set of instructions were given to the Hebrews before the final plague. These instructions are known as "The Feast of Passover", "The Feast of Unleavened Bread", and "The Law of the

Firstborn." In these rituals are displayed the law of sacrifice, the law of the gospel, and the law of consecration, all necessary requirements to receive ultimate salvation from spiritual death. As God's children today we have learned through this mighty demonstration of divine power that ultimately it will require the fear of God to receive salvation from the "One True God."

This brings us to the conclusion of this chapter, I pray that the good Lord blesses you as you respect and honor Him in the mighty name of Jesus, Amen. We shall proceed to the last and final chapter which reveals the relationship between The Passover and Pentecost.

CHAPTER FIFTEEN

The Passover and The Pentecost – Their relationship

Introduction

We shall discuss in this chapter, the relationship between The Passover and The Pentecost. We shall also shed some light on what makes the two connected along with the blessings they both bring, be blessed as you read through in Jesus name, Amen.

What is Pentecost?

Pentecost can be defined as a Christian festival occurring on Whit Sunday commemorating the descent of the Holy Ghost on the apostles of Christ. The term Pentecost comes from the Greek word *Pentēkostē* meaning "fiftieth".

It refers to the Jewish festival celebrated on the fiftieth day after First Fruits, also known as the "Feast of 50 days" in rabbinic tradition.

Furthermore, it is also called the Feast of Weeks, Shavuot, Shavous or Shabuoth. In Judaism, it is the harvest festival celebrated fifty days after the second day of Passover on the sixth and seventh days of Sivan, and commemorating the giving of the Torah on Mount Sinai.

So the Christian High Holy Day of Pentecost is celebrated on the 50th day (the seventh Sunday) from Easter

Sunday. It commemorates the descent of the Holy Spirit upon the Apostles and other followers of Jesus Christ while they were in Jerusalem celebrating the Feast of Weeks, as described in the Acts of the Apostles (Acts 2:1–31).

Acts 2:1-31 (KJV) And when the day of Pentecost was fully come, they were all with one accord in one place.

(2) And suddenly there came a sound from heaven as of a rushing mighty wind, and it filled all the house where they were sitting.

(3) And there appeared unto them cloven tongues like as of fire, and it sat upon each of them.

(4) And they were all filled with the Holy Ghost, and began to speak with other tongues, as the Spirit gave them utterance.

(5) And there were dwelling at Jerusalem Jews, devout men, out of every nation under heaven.

(6) Now when this was noised abroad, the multitude came together, and were confounded, because that every man heard them speak in his own language.

(7) And they were all amazed and marvelled, saying one to another, Behold, are not all these which speak Galilaeans?

(8) And how hear we every man in our own tongue, wherein we were born?

(9) Parthians, and Medes, and Elamites, and the dwellers in Mesopotamia, and in Judaea, and Cappadocia, in Pontus, and Asia

(10) Phrygia, and Pamphylia, in Egypt, and in the parts of Libya about Cyrene, and strangers of Rome, Jews and proselytes,

(11) Cretes and Arabians, we do hear them speak in our tongues the wonderful works of God.

(12) And they were all amazed, and were in doubt, saying one to another, What meaneth this?

(13) Others mocking said, These men are full of new wine.

(14) But Peter, standing up with the eleven, lifted up his voice, and said unto them, Ye men of Judaea, and all ye that dwell at Jerusalem, be this known unto you, and hearken to my words:

(15) For these are not drunken, as ye suppose, seeing it is but the third hour of the day.

(16) But this is that which was spoken by the prophet Joel;

(17) And it shall come to pass in the last days, saith God, I will pour out of my Spirit upon all flesh: and your sons and

*your daughters shall prophesy, and your
young men shall see visions, and your
old men shall dream dreams:*
*(18) And on my servants and on my
handmaidens I will pour out in those
days of my Spirit; and they shall
prophesy:*
*(19) And I will shew wonders in heaven
above, and signs in the earth beneath;
blood, and fire, and vapour of smoke:*
*(20) The sun shall be turned into
darkness, and the moon into blood,
before that great and notable day of the
Lord come:*
*(21) And it shall come to pass, that
whosoever shall call on the name of the
Lord shall be saved.*
*(22) Ye men of Israel, hear these words;
Jesus of Nazareth, a man approved of
God among you by miracles and
wonders and signs, which God did by*

him in the midst of you, as ye yourselves also know:

(23) Him, being delivered by the determinate counsel and foreknowledge of God, ye have taken, and by wicked hands have crucified and slain:

(24) Whom God hath raised up, having loosed the pains of death: because it was not possible that he should be holden of it.

(25) For David speaketh concerning him, I foresaw the Lord always before my face, for he is on my right hand, that I should not be moved:

(26) Therefore did my heart rejoice, and my tongue was glad; moreover also my flesh shall rest in hope:

(27) Because thou wilt not leave my soul in hell, neither wilt thou suffer thine Holy One to see corruption.

*(28) Thou hast made known to me the
ways of life; thou shalt make me full of
joy with thy countenance.*

*(29) Men and brethren, let me freely
speak unto you of the patriarch David,
that he is both dead and buried, and his
sepulchre is with us unto this day.*

*(30) Therefore being a prophet, and
knowing that God had sworn with an
oath to him, that of the fruit of his loins,
according to the flesh, he would raise up
Christ to sit on his throne;*

*(31) He seeing this before spake of the
resurrection of Christ, that his soul was
not left in hell, neither his flesh did see
corruption.*

The Connection

The connection between Jesus' death
on a cross and the Passover is obvious
in multiple places in the New
Testament. Three places are
mentioned here. The first
interactions, recorded in the New
Testament, of John the Baptist and
Jesus are found in chapter one of the
gospel of John.

Which reads:

*John 1:29 (KJV)The next day John
seeth Jesus coming unto him, and saith,
Behold the Lamb of God, which taketh
away the sin of the world.*

The meaning of the above passage
signifies the celebration of Passover.
This holiday looked back to the days
of Moses, when lambs' blood covered

the doors of Israel, and allowed God's judgment to "pass over" them.

The connection to Passover and Pentecost is the primary reason Jesus is referred to as "The Lamb of God." His crucifixion also symbolizes other Old Testament sacrifices. Instead of a lamb however, the sin offering specified in the book of Leviticus is a goat. Lambs were sacrificed in the temple for Passover, but goats were cast out of the camp. Jesus will be taken outside the walls of the city to be sacrificed on the cross.

The second is when Jesus and his disciples observed the Passover meal on the first day of Unleavened Bread at the beginning of the Passover Festival. Jesus transformed the Passover meal into the Lord's Supper

for subsequent Christians. Jesus'
death was the fulfillment to which
the original Passover event pointed.
Matthew 26:26-28 says:

*Matthew 26:26-28 (KJV) And as they
were eating, Jesus took bread, and
blessed it, and brake it, and gave it to the
disciples, and said, Take, eat; this is my
body.*
*(27) And he took the cup, and gave
thanks, and gave it to them, saying,
Drink ye all of it;*
*(28) For this is my blood of the new
testament, which is shed for many for the
remission of sins.*

So to shed more light on the above
passage, the Passover meal was
observed by nearly every Jewish
person as a way of remembering and

celebrating God's rescue of Israel through the blood of the lamb on their doorposts.

Now Jesus is using the elements of the Passover meal to introduce something new. Jesus' words regarding the Pentecost have a connection to a powerful moment between God and the people of Israel during the time of Moses. The blood of animal sacrifices was used to seal an agreement between God and the people. God promised to take care of them, and the people promised to be obedient to all God told them.

The disciples, then, would have grown up knowing that a covenant between God and His people was sealed with the blood of a sacrifice.

Now Jesus has described the wine they are drinking as His blood of the covenant. He says that it is poured out for many for the forgiveness of sins.

Jesus is describing a new agreement—a formal promise—between God and many people. This time, though, the covenant will not be for Israel alone.

It will be for all people who come to God through faith in Jesus. Jesus' blood will be poured out to pay the price for the sin of all who trust in Him. His blood will seal the agreement God is making to forgive the sins of these Christ-followers or "Christians," taking Jesus' death as the payment for their sin.

And now Paul, when writing to the church at Corinth, clearly connected Jesus' death to the Passover. He wrote:

1 Corinthians 5:7-8 (KJV) Purge out therefore the old leaven, that ye may be a new lump, as ye are unleavened. For even Christ our passover is sacrificed for us:
(8) Therefore let us keep the feast, not with old leaven, neither with the leaven of malice and wickedness; but with the unleavened bread of sincerity and truth.

So in the above passage, Paul is using bread metaphors to help his readers understand why they must remove the individual who is committing evil from among them. Paul described sin in the church as leaven that is contaminated. It must be removed or it will infect the whole batch of dough, making the bread worthless. Just as is done with certain breads today, a small piece of an earlier batch of dough would be reserved to "seed" the next batch. Fermenting agents in that piece would be spread around the new dough and continue the cycle. So a small influence, either positive or negative, can grow and become universal.

Here, Paul adjusts the metaphor to one best understood by those familiar with the Jewish Passover. In preparation for that celebration, Jews scour their homes to remove any hint of leaven. They would make and eat, instead, unleavened bread. In addition, they would sacrifice a

Passover lamb and put its blood on their doorposts before eating it.

Paul's metaphor puts the Corinthian Christians in the place of the Passover dough. They must cleanse out all the old leaven and become a new, unleavened piece of dough.

Then Paul says something surprising: He says they are already the unleavened dough. This is true because Christ, the Passover lamb, was sacrificed on the cross to pay for their sins. The leaven has already been removed from them. So Paul is urging them to live up to what they already are, the forgiven and set-apart people of Christ.

These three references to the New Testament which are quite exhaustive, but sufficient to show a connection between the Old Testament Passover and the New Testament crucifixion of Jesus. Regardless of some specific details, it is obvious that Jesus' death on the cross is the fulfillment of the event to which the Passover event points. The main motif is deliverance from bondage. The Israelites were delivered from bondage in Egypt, especially from Pharaoh. The motif of Easter is that God's people are delivered from bondage in a fallen world, especially from Satan.

Ten blessings of Passover

According to Exodus 23, The Passover has 10 blessings, each with unique importance for our transition into the next season and deeper levels of intimacy with Christ. These blessings are:

- **Divine Protection:**

*See, I am sending an angel ahead of you
to guard you along the way and to bring
you to the place I have prepared."
Exodus 23:20 (NIV)*

- **Protection from Enemies
through Positioning and
Alignment**

*"…if you indeed obey His voice and do
all that I speak, then I will be an enemy
to your enemies and an adversary to
your adversaries." Exodus 23:22 (NIV)*

- **Commissioning of Divine
Authority**

*"You shall not bow down to their gods,
nor serve them, nor do according to their*

works; but you shall utterly overthrow them and completely break down their sacred pillars." Exodus 23:24 (NIV)

- **Supernatural Health and Kingdom Prosperity**

"So you shall serve the Lord your God, and He will bless your bread and your water. And I will take sickness away from the midst of you." Exodus 23:25 (NIV)

- **Covenant Protection for Multiplication and Longevity**

"No one shall suffer miscarriage or be barren in your land; I will fulfill the number of your days." Exodus 23:26 (NIV)

- ## A Godly Release of Fear and Respect from Enemies

"I will send My fear before you, I will cause confusion among all the people to whom you come, and will make all your enemies turn their backs to you." Exodus 23:27 (NIV)

- ## Relief from the Threat of Enemies

"And I will send hornets before you, which shall drive out the Hivite, the Canaanite, and the Hittite from before you." Exodus 23:28 (NIV)

- **The Gift of Dominion and an Increased Inheritance:** *"Little by little I will drive them out from before you, until you have increased, and you inherit the land." Exodus 23:30 (NIV)*

- **Freedom from Corrupt Covenants**

"They shall not dwell in your land, lest they make you sin against Me. For if you serve their gods, it will surely be a snare to you." Exodus 23:33 (NIV).

- **Give a special year of blessing**

"I will not drive them out from before thee in one year; lest the land become

*desolate, and the beast of the field
multiply against thee. Exodus 23:29"
(NIV)*

Seven blessings of Pentecost

Pentecost is one of three "Appointed
Times" described in Exodus 23 and
Leviticus 23 as special seasons when
God wants to meet with His people
and bless them in extraordinary
ways. Along with the Feast of
Passover and Feast of Tabernacles,
God instructed His children to
celebrate Pentecost as a perpetual
feast, for all generations (Leviticus
23:40-41).

*Leviticus 23:40-41 (KJV) And ye shall
take you on the first day the boughs of
goodly trees, branches of palm trees, and*

the boughs of thick trees, and willows of the brook; and ye shall rejoice before the LORD your God seven days.

(41) And ye shall keep it a feast unto the LORD seven days in the year. It shall be a statute forever in your generations: ye shall celebrate it in the seventh month.

- ## Baptized with the Holy Spirit

Acts 1:2-5 (KJV) Until the day in which he was taken up, after that he through the Holy Ghost had given commandments unto the apostles whom he had chosen: (3)To whom also he shewed himself alive after his passion by many infallible proofs, being seen of them forty days, and speaking of the

*things pertaining to the kingdom of
God: (4)And, being assembled together
with them, commanded them that they
should not depart from Jerusalem, but
wait for the promise of the Father,
which, saith he, ye have heard of me.
(5)For John truly baptized with water;
but ye shall be baptized with the Holy
Ghost not many days hence.*

- ## Filled with the Holy Spirit

*As part of the fulfillment of Joel's
prophecy, "I will pour out my Spirit on
all people", the infilling of the Spirit is
available to all followers of Jesus. For
this reason Paul is able to say, "you have
been given fullness in Christ",
Col.2:10 (KJV)*

- ## Other Tongues

*Acts 2:4 (KJV) And they were all filled
with the Holy Ghost, and began to speak
with other tongues, as the Spirit gave
them utterance.*

- ## Renewal and restoration

*I will repay you for the years the locusts
have eaten— the great locust and the
young locust, the other locusts and the
locust swarm— my great army that I
sent among you. You will have plenty to
eat, until you are full, and you will
praise the name of the LORD your
God, who has worked wonders for you;
never again will my people be shamed.*

Then you will know that I am in Israel, that I am the LORD your God, and that there is no other; never again my people be shamed. (Joel 2:25-27) (KJV)

- ## A day of blessing and salvation

And afterwards, I will pour out my Spirit on all people. Your sons and daughters will prophesy, your old men will dream dreams, your young men will see visions. Even on my servants, both men and women, I will pour out my Spirit in those days. ... And everyone who calls on the name of the LORD will be saved. (Joel 2 26-29,32) (KJV)

- You will not die before your
  appointed time

*Psalms 118:17 (KJV) I shall not die,
but live, and declare the works of the
LORD*

- An angel of God will be
  assigned to protect you and
  lead you to your miracles

*Exodus 23:20 (KJV) Behold, I send an
Angel before thee, to keep thee in the
way, and to bring thee into the place
which I have prepared.*

God's will be done – The power and purpose of Pentecost and Passover

As we conclude this chapter, its quite evident that it is the will of the Father to grant us his wonderful promises for our deliverance which are healing, provision, and blessings. However, almost every promise in His Word is conditional and based on obedience. God usually says, *"If you do this…I'll do that."*

That's why many believers end up disappointed and disillusioned when they don't see the fulfillment of the Lord's promises and blessings in their life. They're waiting for Him to fulfill His promises, while He's waiting for them to obey an instruction He's given them.

The Pentecost is regarded as a powerful celebration and a reminder that the Holy Spirit came with Divine might to empower our witness to the Risen Christ. It is also the perfect time to remind believers in our church that our Heavenly Father will empower our witness.

Furthermore, the festival of Pentecost is still important to Christians today because it represents the beginning of the Christian Church. It reminds us how Jesus' promise that God would send the Holy Spirit was fulfilled.

Now regarding the Feast of Passover, God promised His children: *"I will bring you out...I will rid you out of bondage...I will redeem you" (Exodus 6:5-6) (KJV).*

But the story didn't end there. The Lord gave His people detailed instructions for how they would gain freedom from their slavery.

So the Passover celebration is gravely important in the lives of we Christians today because it underscores powerful themes of strength, hope, and triumph over both spiritual and physical adversity.

God made it clear in the scriptures that this was to be a time of new beginnings: *"This month shall be unto you beginning of months; it shall be the first month of the year to you" (Exodus 12:1-2) (KJV)*. However, notice that when God spoke these words, the Israelites were still living as slaves in the land of Egypt.

They clearly needed a new beginning—and perhaps you do as well, I pray that the Lord our God will bestow upon us all, a new dawn filled with blessings from above in the mighty name of Jesus, Amen.

Altar call to receive Christ

The greatest blessing, we can receive from our Lord in heaven is the blessing of salvation.

To receive this, you must surrender your life to Jesus and accept Him as your Lord and personal saviour.

If you would like to do so now, kindly say this prayer with your whole heart.

"Dear Lord Jesus Christ, Thank you for dying for the remission of my sins on the cross of Calvary.

The Power and Purpose of The Passover and Pentecost

I believe you are the son of God, that you died for my sins, were   buried and rose on the third day and the you are seated at the right hand of Our father in heaven.

I believe you will come back again to take the saints to heaven.

With my heart I believe these things and that you are my Lord and personal Saviour.

Please forgive me my sins and I also forgive others right now because you first forgave me and if I don't forgive, you won't forgive me either. Write my name in the book of life.

Come into my life and become my Lord and personal saviour.

With my mouth I confess that you are my Lord and saviour of my soul

Fill me with your Holy Spirit and grant me the grace to lead a life righteousness, holiness and of fire.

In Jesus Christ name I pray, Amen."

If you prayed this prayer and really meant it, I Believe you have received the miracle of salvation

Prayerfully seek a Bible believing, Holy Spirit filled Church and become a member there.

Ask them to baptize you and teach you the ways of Christ.

Or contact us if you need guideline.

Prayer Points for Passover

1. O God, let the fire of revival, fall upon the Rapha Christian Centre, in the name of Jesus.

2. O God, arise and give us God-fearing leaders, in the name of Jesus.

3. Father, we confess and repent of the sins that opened the door for this pestilence, in the name of Jesus.

4. O Lord, let Your mercy speak and have mercy upon us as a nation, in Jesus' name.

5. We bind and cast out the crowned dragon from the East out of our land, in the name of Jesus.

6. Power of the Most High, overshadow those seeking for cure and prevention, in the name of Jesus.

7. Divine immunity, by the blood of Jesus, overshadow all our health workers, in the name of Jesus.

8. O Lord, grant our leaders divine wisdom to manage this crisis, in the name of Jesus

9. We command the air to vomit all the seeds and tokens of death it has harboured, in the name of Jesus.

10. Thank You, Father for the benefits and provision of the blood of Jesus.

11. The wall of the blood of Jesus is around me and my household, any evil force that comes near us shall catch fire, in the name of Jesus.

12. Passover blood of Jesus, envelope our nation, in the name of Jesus.

13. Passover blood of Jesus, envelope our land, in the name of Jesus.

14. Passover blood of Jesus, envelope me and my family, in the name of Jesus.

15. By the power in the blood of Jesus, we stop the spread of this pandemic, in the name of Jesus.

16. I draw a circle of the blood of Jesus around me against every arrow of infirmity, in the name of Jesus.

17. I overcome every spirit of infirmity by the blood of the Lamb, in the name of Jesus.

18. I apply the blood of Jesus to every hidden sickness in my life, in the name of Jesus.

19. Let the blood of Jesus speak confusion into the camp of the enemy, in the name of Jesus.

20. Let the blood of Jesus speak peace unto every organ in my body, in the name of Jesus.

21. Let the blood of Jesus minister defeat to every evil work in my life, in the name of Jesus.

22. Blood of Jesus, speak better things into my life, in the name of Jesus.

23. I bind and cast out all spirits of fear, in the name of Jesus.

24. Let the power of salvation and healing overshadow our nation, in the name of Jesus.

Prayer Points for Pentecost

1. Lord of the Harvest, You gave Your disciples the mandate to be Your witnesses around the world and empowered them with Your Holy Spirit on the day of Pentecost to accomplish this task. Today, we ask that You help us to refocus our attention, as we face a task unfinished. You have blessed us with the power and the gifts of Your Holy Spirit. Help us to use these for ministry and witness. Amen.

2. God of Wind and Fire, we celebrate today the indwelling of Your Holy Spirit, which You sent upon the believers on the day of Pentecost, and which is our blessing today. Lord, we thank You for the transforming work of Your Holy

Spirit in our lives and through our lives toward others. We thank You that You have given us boldness to proclaim the Gospel. Remind us to use Your power to do the work You have given us. Amen.

3. Breath of Life, on this Pentecost Sunday, we ask that You breathe on us once again. Make our consciences tender to Your touch. We hunger for the life-changing power that Your Holy Spirit brings. May our lives exemplify the fruit of Your Spirit: love, joy, peace, patience, kindness, goodness, faithfulness, gentleness, and self-control. May we use the gifts of the Spirit that You have distributed to bless the church and build Your Kingdom on earth. Amen.

4. Joy of Heaven, we are so blessed that You came to dwell in each of us on Pentecost, when Your church was born. Surely, through Your Spirit, we have died to sin and are alive to holiness. May we serve You faithfully, in praise, prayer, and loving service to others, as we are changed from glory to glory. May we walk as children of the light, in all goodness, righteousness, and truth. Amen.

5. Lord of Power, just as the outpouring of Your Holy Spirit on Pentecost so drastically changed the lives of the disciples, may the burning fire of Your Holy Spirit refine and renew us, so that we will never be the same. May we move in the power of the Spirit, and may our lives and ministries be infused with

Your divine, supernatural touch and authority. May the Spirit of Wisdom and Revelation cause us to grow in our knowledge of You. Amen.

6. Living God, thank You for the surpassing greatness of Your power to us who believe. Because You came to dwell in us on Pentecost, we have Your mighty strength with which You raised Christ from the dead. Strengthen us in our inner being, so that we can know the love of Christ that surpasses knowledge and be filled with all the fullness of God. Amen.

Reference list

*Erin B. A brief history of Passover,
which honors resilience amid adversity,
April 7, 2020,*

*https://www.nationalgeographic.com/h
istory/article/history-passover-honors-
resilience-amid-adversity*

*Lesli W. What is Pentecost and Why
Do We Celebrate It?, 2021,*

*https://www.beliefnet.com/faiths/religi
ous-observances/what-is-pentecost-
and-why-do-we-celebrate-it.aspx*

*"List of Egyptian deities." Wikipedia,
Wikimedia Foundation, June 2021,*

*https://en.m.wikipedia.org/wiki/List
of_Egyptian_deities*

The Power and Purpose of The Passover and Pentecost

"Passover." Wikipedia, Wikimedia Foundation, June 2021,

https://en.m.wikipedia.org/wiki/Passover

"Pentecost." Wikipedia, Wikimedia Foundation, June 2021,

https://en.m.wikipedia.org/wiki/Pentecost

Ronald T. Passover and Pentecost, 2012,

http://www.rtconstant.com/essays/religion/PassoverPentecost.pdf

"Ten Egyptian Plagues For Ten Egyptian Gods and Goddesses." Stat.rice.edu, 2021,

The Power and Purpose of The Passover and Pentecost

http://www.stat.rice.edu/~dobelman/D inotech/10_Egyptian_gods_10_Plague s.pdf

About the Author

Bishop Dr. Joseph C. Kanu has a medical background but was called by God to serve Him drastically through several visions, dreams, Prophecies and Confirmations.

He resisted God's calling for as long as he could but had to surrender to God's will in 2012 in London United Kingdom when God allowed every other door in his life to become shut but left the door to God's house open to him.

He attended Bible School in London United Kingdom. He has an honorary doctorate for his accomplishments in God's kingdom. He also holds the title: Defender of the faith and other titles. He was set apart as a Bishop Elect and later consecrated into the office of a Bishop by the College of Bishops in London United Kingdom.

He is a Song Writer, Singer and Worshipper. He has written and produced his own songs and albums such as: Reggae Praise Medley, Redemption blood, Worship Medley Experience, The Man of Galilee, Praise Experience Medley, Your name is Rapha and Don't give up on Jesus (Rap Song).

He is also an intercessor and has produced
My prayer and prophecies for you (Audio).

He has also written several other books. Such as:

- Making room for your miracles. (Lessons from the Shunamite)

- How to hear from God everyday

- The Unfamiliar Touch
  (Lesson from the woman with the issue of blood).

- Living everyday under open heavens
  (lessons from Jacob's life)

- The Ministerial offices
  (Ethics and Etiquettes)

- Prayers That Availeth much

- Passover and Pentecost
  (Their Power and Purpose)

He was ordained as an Evangelist in London and later on as a Pastor In Assemblies of God Church. He has served and trained as a minister in different churches such as RCCG, AG, BLW CFAN to mention but a few.

He was personally trained and imparted by the Late Evangelist Reinhard Bonke and his team when he was a student of his school of Evangelism in London.

He also received impartation and teaching from Benny Hinn, and late Morris Cerrulo to mention but a few

He runs School of Supernatural Ministry in London where he teaches and equips ministers to move in the Supernatural.
He is the presiding Bishop of Rapha Christian Centre house of Healing London and also the President of Bishop Joseph Global Ministries.

He travels the world with the message of God's kingdom, demonstrating the power of God in the Prophetic, Healing, Miraculous and Deliverance Ministries.

He is married to a British Citizen from South America/ Carribean Island Of Barbados and they are blessed with children.

Contact Details

Bishop Dr. Joseph C. Kanu

Presiding Bishop Rapha Christian Centre house of Healing London

And President of Bishop Joseph Global Ministries

36 Pitlake Croydon

London United Kingdom

Cr0 3RA

+4478 31 62 52 42

Email: Bishopjosephkanu@gmail.com

www.ingramcontent.com/pod-product-compliance
Lightning Source LLC
LaVergne TN
LVHW011350080426
835511LV00005B/228